Original title:
When I Rise

Copyright © 2024 Swan Charm
All rights reserved.

Author: Paula Raudsepp
ISBN HARDBACK: 978-9916-89-745-4
ISBN PAPERBACK: 978-9916-89-746-1
ISBN EBOOK: 978-9916-89-747-8

Wings of the Beloved

In shadows deep, Your light does shine,
With whispers soft, I feel divine.
Grace carries me on gentle wings,
In Your embrace, my spirit sings.

Every prayer a feather bright,
Lifting hearts to sacred height.
In stillness, hear the angels call,
With love that breaks each binding thrall.

Through valleys low, and mountains high,
Your presence is my steadfast sky.
A journey dressed in faith and hope,
With every step, in You I cope.

Let mercy flow like rivers wide,
In Your protection, I will bide.
Each challenge faced, a lesson earned,
In fire's glow, my spirit burned.

Oh, Beloved, lift me higher still,
For in Your love, I've found my will.
With every breath, I seek Your grace,
In gratitude, I find my place.

The Celestial Rise

In dawn's first light, the heavens burst,
With every star, a sacred thirst.
The cosmos sings of love so pure,
In faith, our hearts will always endure.

Lift your eyes to the endless skies,
Where every dream and hope arise.
A tapestry of souls entwined,
In unity, our spirits bind.

Through storms that roar and shadows long,
In trials faced, our hearts grow strong.
With every tear, a seed is sown,
In love's embrace, we are not alone.

Let kindness flow like rivers clear,
Embrace the lost, hold every dear.
For in the light of grace divine,
We share our paths, together shine.

As day gives way to evening's grace,
We find our peace in time and space.
A celestial rise, our spirits soar,
In love's embrace, forevermore.

Spirits Uplifted by Grace

In the shadow of His light, we rise,
He whispers truth, lifts our sighs.
Grace flows like rivers, pure and wide,
With each heartbeat, our spirits abide.

In stillness, we find our peace,
A sacred promise that will not cease.
He guides our steps on paths so right,
Filling our souls with holy light.

Within the temple of our hearts,
Love's gentle song, the greatest art.
In prayer, our burdens fade away,
We walk in joy, by night and day.

With every tear, His hands we feel,
A balm to soothe, a love to heal.
In fellowship, we gather near,
Our voices raised, dispelling fear.

Through trials faced and storms endured,
In faith, our lives are reassured.
Uplifted, we stand, united and bold,
In the warmth of grace, our stories told.

Journey to Celestial Heights

We embark on this sacred quest,
With humble hearts, we seek the best.
Each step we take, a prayer in motion,
To ascend with love, deep as the ocean.

Mountains tall and valleys low,
Through faith's embrace, we learn to grow.
In every trial, a lesson found,
A sweet whisper of grace abound.

The stars above, they shine with grace,
Our souls are touched in this vast space.
With courage bright, we raise our gaze,
Towards the light, our spirits blaze.

Hand in hand, we climb the way,
Through darkest night, we find the day.
In unity, our hearts ignite,
Together we soar, to heaven's height.

As we journey, we cast aside,
The fears and doubts that seek to hide.
On wings of prayer, our dreams take flight,
To reach the heavens, a glorious sight.

The Morning Starlight of Belief

When dawn breaks with His radiant grace,
We rise anew, light on our face.
With starlit dreams that guide our way,
Belief awakens with each new day.

In the hush of morn, our hearts align,
With whispered truths, divine and fine.
Hope blooms softly with the sun,
In every moment, His love's begun.

Through trials faced, our faith stands firm,
In darkest trials, love's light will burn.
For every doubt, a choice to see,
The beauty held in unity.

The morning starlight, a gentle beam,
Awakens our souls, revives each dream.
With every heartbeat, we grow more aware,
Embracing all that leads us there.

So let us walk with heads held high,
For in our hearts, the heavens lie.
With faith as our guide, we shall achieve,
The magic found in hearts that believe.

A Heart Transformed in Worship

In the quiet of the night, we kneel,
A heart laid bare, our souls reveal.
With whispers soft, we seek His grace,
In sacred stillness, we find our place.

Each prayer a note, our spirits sing,
A melody of love the angels bring.
Through trials faced, our hearts unite,
In worship's glow, we seek the light.

With lifted hands, our burdens shed,
In surrender, every fear is dead.
A transformation, pure and divine,
In worship's warmth, our lives align.

As shadows flee and hope is reignited,
In every heartbeat, we are united.
With every song, our spirits soar,
In worship's embrace, we long for more.

A heart transformed through grace, we see,
In love's embrace, we truly free.
With joy, we walk, in faith secure,
In worship's glow, we shall endure.

Wings of Faith

On wings of faith, we soar so high,
With hearts aflame, we touch the sky.
In trials faced, we find our grace,
In every step, the Lord's embrace.

Each whispered prayer, a gentle guide,
Through stormy seas, He shall abide.
With courage found in sacred light,
We walk in love, the path of right.

The Call of the Morning

Awake, arise, the morning calls,
In radiant light, His promise falls.
The world awaits, His truth to share,
In every heart, His burdens bear.

With every dawn, new hope breaks free,
In sweet communion, God and we.
The gentle breeze, His voice divine,
Through nature's grace, our spirits shine.

From Darkness to Glory

From darkness deep, we seek the light,
With faith ablaze, we rise in might.
In shadows lost, we find our way,
Toward brighter tomorrows, we shall sway.

Each life redeemed, a story told,
In every heart, His love unfolds.
Through trials faced, our spirits grown,
In sacred truth, we are not lone.

A Higher Calling

The heavens sing, a higher call,
In whispered winds, we hear it all.
With open hearts, we heed His word,
In every moment, a chance unheard.

Through paths unknown, we venture forth,
In unity, we find our worth.
With hands entwined, we pledge to serve,
In faith and love, we shall preserve.

Celestial Awakening

In the dawn's embrace, light does break,
Heaven whispers softly, for our sake.
Stars bow to the rising sun's ray,
Guiding our hearts to a brighter way.

The hymn of creation fills the air,
Angels sing of love, pure and fair.
Mountaintops rise, spirits take flight,
In this sacred moment, all feels right.

With every breath, we sense the grace,
Divine presence wrapped in time and space.
Nature dances to the holy call,
In celestial realms, we stand tall.

Prayers lift like incense to the skies,
In stillness, we witness the world rise.
Together, we journey, hand in hand,
Awakened by love's eternal command.

Hope is reborn in every heart,
Transforming shadows, fear departs.
In this awakening, we see the Light,
Celestial harmony, shining bright.

From Ashes to Ascendance

In the depths of despair, a spark ignites,
Faith's resilience transforms latest fights.
From the ashes, a spirit shall soar,
Rising anew, to be lost nevermore.

With every trial, our strength refines,
Hearts meld as one, in sacred designs.
The journey through darkness brings forth the flame,
From suffering's grip, we rise in His name.

Forgiveness rains down, a blessed gift,
From burdens heavied, our spirits we lift.
In unity we stand, side by side,
Through valleys of pain, we shall abide.

Like the phoenix, through flames we ascend,
Embracing the road, on God we depend.
Transformed in the fire, we shine so bright,
In this journey of love, we find our light.

Through trials and storms, we shall not sway,
For in each struggle, we learn to pray.
From ashes, we walk, hand in hand,
To the heights of His grace, as we stand.

The Promise of the New Day

Morning breaks with promise anew,
Each ray of sunlight speaks truth to you.
With each dawn's glow, hope rekindles,
In the heart's quiet, faith gently tingles.

The sun rises high, casting away dread,
In the warmth of love, the spirit is fed.
Every moment breathed feels sacred and rare,
Promises whispered in the morning air.

Together, we gather in light's embrace,
Worshiping grace in this holy space.
With open hearts, we rise to pray,
Each moment a blessing, come what may.

Mountains before us will fade from sight,
With the promise of dawn, we find our might.
A new day beckons, take each step bold,
In the promise of love, unity unfolds.

Gently we walk on this path divine,
In faith and hope, our souls intertwine.
Fear no longer holds, joy shall reign,
For every new day is God's grand domain.

The Spirit's Soaring Flight

Oh, the spirit lifts on wings so free,
Transcending the earth to eternity.
In the realm of the Divine, we take flight,
Guided by love's ever-radiant light.

Like doves that ascend through heavens wide,
In peaceful surrender, we abide.
With every heartbeat, our souls embrace,
The essence of life, wrapped in His grace.

Mountains may tremble and oceans may roar,
Yet in His presence, we seek evermore.
With trust as our anchor, our fears release,
Through every trial, we find our peace.

In prayerful whispers, our spirits unite,
Soaring together in the twilight.
For love is the flame that ignites the night,
In the spirit's soaring, we find our might.

With open hearts, let the journey unfold,
In the spirit's flight, we break every mold.
With grace we soar, through clouds of strife,
Living the promise of eternal life.

The Spirit's Ascent

In silence, we lift our hearts high,
To the heavens beyond our sight.
Faith leads us through the night,
In trust we find our light.

Wings of hope safely embrace,
With grace, we journey on.
Each step a sacred trace,
In the dawn, we are reborn.

Through trials, our spirits soar,
As we rise towards His love.
Each prayer opens a door,
To the blessings from above.

In communion, we find peace,
As we seek the holy call.
All burdens cease to increase,
In His mercy, we stand tall.

A symphony of voices raised,
United in the divine plan.
By His grace, we are amazed,
Together, as one, we can.

The Path of Surrender

In humility, we lay it down,
The weight of our own desire.
With open hearts, we wear the crown,
Of surrender's sacred fire.

In trust, we walk this narrow way,
Guided by the light within.
The shadows fade, they cannot stay,
For love's journey does begin.

Each step leads us closer still,
To the promise of His grace.
In quiet, we align our will,
With the beauty of His face.

As we give up our control,
The spirit dances free.
In letting go, we find our soul,
In unison, we see.

With open hands, we trust the flow,
Of wisdom that is divine.
Our hearts will bloom and overflow,
In the love that is sublime.

Rising with the Sun

Each morning brings a new embrace,
The dawn awakens our belief.
With joy, we greet the sacred space,
Where grace replaces all our grief.

The sunlight bathes our weary souls,
Renewing hope with every ray.
In unity, our spirit rolls,
And guides us through the day.

As nature sings its hymn of light,
We rise with gratitude in hand.
In every shadow, find the bright,
For love is our promised land.

In the warmth, we find our peace,
All worries begin to fade.
As blessings flow, our joys increase,
In His name, we are remade.

To the rhythm of the day we dance,
In harmony with all creation.
Each moment, a divine chance,
To live in joyful celebration.

The Breath of New Beginnings

In the stillness, hear the call,
A whisper of love in the air.
With every breath, we stand tall,
Embracing grace, casting despair.

As seasons change, so do we,
Transforming pain into peace.
From the ashes, we are free,
In His hands, we find release.

Every heartbeat is divine,
A sacred rhythm in the night.
Through our struggles, we align,
With the promise of pure light.

In blessings small and great we find,
The beauty of creation's hand.
In every soul, His love entwined,
Together, we shall stand.

With faith, we rise anew each day,
A canvas for His love to write.
With every breath, we humbly pray,
To live in eternal light.

Abounding in Grace

In the morning light, we rise,
Filled with grace from skies above.
Hearts alight with holy praise,
Bound together, we seek His love.

In the trials that we face,
God's mercy wraps us near.
Each tear we shed, a sacred trace,
Whispers hope, dispels our fear.

With every step, His presence near,
Guiding paths we cannot see.
In faith we walk, our purpose clear,
For in His arms, we are free.

Through shadows dark and nights so long,
A light shines, our souls embrace.
In unity, we sing our song,
A testament to His grace.

When the world feels cold and grim,
We gather close, love does prevail.
Our hearts are filled, the light won't dim,
In God's embrace, we shall not fail.

Triumph of the Spirit

From ashes rise the spirits bold,
In trials strong, our faith takes flight.
With courage bright, our hearts unfold,
Guided by love, we claim the light.

In every storm, a moment found,
Resilient souls, we stand and fight.
His grace, our anchor, always sound,
We soar on wings, in endless height.

With every breath, the victory sings,
A dance of joy beneath the skies.
In unity, our spirit clings,
Together we rise, each heart complies.

In the silence, hear the call,
Of hope restored, a dream anew.
In love's embrace, we stand tall,
Through trials faced, our strength rings true.

As dawn breaks forth, we claim our place,
Triumph's banner waves on high.
Eternal love, our saving grace,
With faithful hearts, we touch the sky.

A Covenant of Hope

In the stillness of the night,
We ponder promises made true.
Hearts united, souls take flight,
In every hope, His love shines through.

Through valleys deep and mountains tall,
We walk the path, hand in hand.
In trials faced, we hear His call,
Together strong, we make our stand.

With stars that guide our weary way,
A beacon bright, a gentle light.
In faith we rise, our spirits sway,
For in His arms, we find our might.

As seasons change, His word remains,
A steadfast rock, our refuge dear.
With joy we dance, despite the rains,
In covenant, we cast out fear.

When shadows loom, and doubts arise,
We hold to hope with hearts aflame.
Together we will reach the skies,
In every breath, we praise His name.

Illuminated Horizons

Across the plains where grace unfolds,
We seek the light that leads the way.
With open hearts and hands to hold,
In faith, we step into the day.

The sun arises, casting dreams,
A tapestry of hope and love.
Through every trial, His light beams,
Guiding us as peace descends from above.

When shadows dance and fears encroach,
His presence calms the stormy sea.
With every whisper, He'll encroach,
Reminding us we're truly free.

In every breath, the promise shines,
A horizon bright, our hearts aspire.
Together, strong, we draw the lines,
Where love ignites an endless fire.

So let us rise with one accord,
In unity, we thrive and sing.
Our spirits soar with one brave word,
In hope, together we take wing.

Graceful Ascent to the Divine

Upon the mountain, shadows thrum,
Hearts aglow, where spirits come.
In fragrant winds, the prayers rise,
A pathway woven 'neath the skies.

With hands uplifted, voices blend,
In harmony, our souls intend.
The light descends, a golden thread,
Uniting all, in love we're led.

In silence deep, the moments flow,
Each breath a step, the grace we know.
Transcending fears, we chant in peace,
A glimpse of hope, our soul's release.

Upon this journey, stars surround,
In unity, we stand profound.
Together, hearts in song we raise,
A celebration of Your grace.

So let us climb this sacred height,
To touch the heart of endless light.
In reverence, we seek and find,
A graceful ascent of heart and mind.

The Tapestry of Faith Unfurls

In twilight's glow, the weavers toil,
With threads of hope, their dreams uncoil.
Each stitch a prayer, each knot a sign,
In every fold, Your love divine.

The colors bright, each shade a plea,
A canvas vast, for all to see.
In sacred patterns, life entwined,
A tapestry of hearts aligned.

The hands that labor, woven tight,
Bear witness to the endless light.
Through trials faced, through joys we share,
Each woven strand, a story rare.

Together, threads of grace we weave,
In faith's embrace, we will believe.
With open hearts, we craft our fate,
In life's grand loom, we celebrate.

The tapestry unfolds in time,
A portrait of the love sublime.
In every heart, Your truth unfurls,
A masterpiece that faith unfurls.

Rising with Angels in Praise

In dawn's soft light, we lift our song,
With angels' voices, we belong.
Their wings outspread, in love they soar,
Together, we unite for more.

With every note, the heavens dance,
In sacred rhythms, we take a chance.
Echoes of grace fill the air,
A bond of joy, beyond compare.

Through trials faced, our spirits climb,
In unity, we find our rhyme.
Hand in hand, we rise in prayer,
With angels close, our praises share.

Each heartbeat sings, a sacred thread,
In harmony, our spirits spread.
With every breath, we honor the light,
As angels guide us through the night.

So let us rise, our voices free,
In perfect union, jubilee.
With angels near, our hearts ablaze,
Together we'll lift, in joyful praise.

The Divine Whisper of the Dawn

In early light, a whisper stirs,
Soft as the breeze, in heart it purrs.
In colors bright, the day awakes,
A promise held, no fear it shakes.

Through stillness deep, the Spirit speaks,
A gentle touch, the comfort seeks.
As sunbeams break, our worries cease,
In morning's glow, we find our peace.

The shadows flee at love's embrace,
In every soul, Your warmth we trace.
With grateful hearts, we seek to find,
The whispered truths, the ties that bind.

As flowers bloom, in vibrant grace,
We gather strength in this sacred space.
Through trials faced, we walk as one,
With each new dawn, our hope begun.

So let us heed that soft refrain,
In every joy, in every pain.
For in the dawn, a promise stays,
A divine whisper guides our ways.

To the Mountain of Grace

O Mountain high, where blessings flow,
In silent whispers, hearts do glow.
Each step we climb, in faith we rise,
As skies unfold with promise lies.

In every shadow, light will gleam,
As souls are anchored in the dream.
On paths adorned with love's embrace,
We find our peace in sacred space.

The winds of hope, they guide our way,
With every prayer, we humbly stay.
The summit calls with gentle sigh,
To dwell in grace, where angels fly.

With eager hearts and yearning cries,
We seek the truth that never dies.
Each moment spent, a sacred trust,
In faith we walk, in love we must.

O Mountain tall, we journey forth,
To find our worth in heavenly worth.
At journey's end, we'll find the face,
Of love divine in mountain grace.

A Soul's Ascent towards Glory

Awake, dear soul, to morning's light,
A journey calls, in spirit's flight.
With every heartbeat, rise and seek,
The path of love, the truth we speak.

Through valleys deep, through forests wide,
With every tear, our hearts abide.
In trials faced and shadows cast,
We find our strength, our faith held fast.

The call of glory, soft and sweet,
In every moment, love we greet.
As stars align and skies unfold,
Our spirits rise, our stories told.

In unity, we strive and yearn,
Through prayers ascended, hearts will burn.
With courage woven in each breath,
We seek the light beyond our death.

A soul transformed, in glory's grace,
We rise as one, embrace the space.
The heavens open, shining bright,
In love's ascent, we find our light.

Rising on Wings of Prayer

Oh Spirit guide, on wings of prayer,
In silent moments, we declare.
With every whisper, love unfolds,
A holy truth that never molds.

The weight of worry, we release,
In every prayer, we find our peace.
Through trials faced and storms that roar,
We rise on wings, forevermore.

In hands uplifted, hearts set free,
We seek Your light, O Sanctity.
With every dawn, a chance to start,
To soar above, united heart.

As desires bloom like flowers bright,
We lean on faith, embrace the light.
Through whispers soft and hymns that sing,
We rise in grace, with love we bring.

The skies rejoice, as prayers ascend,
In unity, we find our blend.
With hope eternal, let us dare,
To rise on wings, on wings of prayer.

Through Trials, I Ascend

Through trials faced, my spirit strong,
In darkest nights, I find my song.
With every challenge, I will stand,
For strength is found in faith's command.

The road may twist, the path unkind,
Yet love's pure light will guide my mind.
With open heart, I press ahead,
In every step, by grace I'm led.

The mountains rise, the valleys low,
Yet still I rise, my spirit's glow.
With every tear, a lesson learned,
For through the fire, my heart has burned.

In faith I trust, in hope I soar,
Each trial faced, I'll love once more.
The trials pass, but love will stay,
Through every night, towards brighter day.

And as I climb, I find my peace,
In love's embrace, sweet, pure release.
So through the trials, I ascend,
To where my soul shall meet its end.

The Veil of Night Lifted

In shadows deep where silence dwells,
The dawn breaks forth, a sound compels.
With whispers soft, the spirits soar,
And light emerges evermore.

Morning's grace, a sacred sign,
Illuminating hearts divine.
The veil of night, it fades away,
Revealing truth in bright array.

A chorus sings of hope restored,
In every heart, a sacred chord.
As day begets a brand new chance,
We join the light in holy dance.

Together we, in faith abide,
With open hearts, our souls reside.
In every moment, love's embrace,
The veil of night—a fleeting face.

Echoes of the Divine Dawn

In the quiet, the spirit sighs,
Awakened now, our souls arise.
The gentle breeze, a guiding hand,
Leads us forth in promised land.

Each step we take, a prayer we weave,
In every breath, the heart believes.
The morning calls in sacred tone,
Through light and love, we are not alone.

The world ignites with colors bright,
A canvas painted in pure light.
Echoes of grace resound anew,
In every heartbeat, love shines through.

We gather in the warmth of day,
In gratitude, we humbly stay.
With open arms, we give and share,
Embracing all with tender care.

The Pilgrimage Within

A journey starts in sacred space,
Where silence holds a warm embrace.
Within the heart, the compass beats,
To guide us through and show us feats.

Each step unfolds a path of light,
Through shadows cast in lost twilight.
In every trial, we seek to learn,
As flames of faith ignite and burn.

A whispered prayer, a gentle thought,
With every breath, a lesson sought.
In solitude, we find our song,
To listen close where we belong.

The pilgrimage is not alone,
In every heart, full love is grown.
We walk in faith, our spirits raised,
A journey blessed and set ablaze.

Ascending through Prayer

We gather here in sacred trust,
With voices joined, in love we must.
Through prayerful hearts, we seek the skies,
In every word, our spirit flies.

The mountains high, the valleys deep,
In prayer we climb, in faith we leap.
Each supplication, a sacred plea,
Unveiling all that's meant to be.

With hands held high, we lift our dreams,
In light we find eternal themes.
Ascending through the grace of night,
We shine like stars, embracing light.

In harmony, our hearts align,
A song of life, divine design.
Through prayer, we rise and share the bliss,
In love eternal, a holy kiss.

Alighting from the Depths

From shadows deep we seek the light,
In faith we rise, dispelling night.
Each prayer a step, each breath a vow,
Emerging forth, transformed somehow.

With heavy hearts, we cast aside,
The burdens borne, our faith our guide.
In sacred whispers, hope ignites,
We find our way through endless nights.

The waters calm, the skies break clear,
Divine embrace, we draw so near.
With every trial, our souls now gleam,
Awakening through the holy dream.

As dawn unfolds its gentle grace,
The depths recede, we find our place.
In unity, our spirits soar,
To heights unknown, forevermore.

With gratitude, we lift our voice,
In harmony, we make our choice.
The path revealed, in love we tread,
Alighting from the depths, we're led.

Stirrings of the Celestial Soul

Awake, O heart, from slumber deep,
The stars above in silence weep.
In every beat, divine refrain,
Stirrings rise, a sacred gain.

In whispered winds, the spirits call,
Through earthly trials, we shall not fall.
Each pulse of life, a chance to shine,
To touch the heavenly, pure, divine.

In parables of ancient lore,
The sacred truths we must explore.
With faith as guide, we seek the way,
To find the light in every day.

From depths of sorrow, rise and sing,
To every moment, joy we bring.
With open hearts, we lift our face,
Embrace the love, the boundless grace.

As stars align, our spirits blend,
In unity, the souls ascend.
The celestial dance, we now partake,
In stirrings bright, our hearts awake.

The Lifting of Heavy Spirits

When shadows loom and burdens press,
We seek the light, our souls confess.
With every tear, a prayer we raise,
To mend the heart in hopeful praise.

The trials faced, though harsh they seem,
In faith we find a brighter dream.
In gentle hands, the sorrows rest,
We rise again, the journey blessed.

Through valleys low, the Spirit guides,
In every heart, the love abides.
As clouds disperse and dawn appears,
The lifting grace dissolves our fears.

In sacred spaces, light unbinds,
The weight of worry, hope unwinds.
Together, we embrace the swell,
The lifting spirits, all is well.

With every heartbeat, joy returns,
In unity, our passion burns.
The dance of life, forever flows,
The heavy lifted, love bestows.

A Journey towards Sacred Abode

With weary feet, we start this quest,
In search of peace, our hearts at rest.
Through mountains high and valleys low,
A journey grand, our spirits grow.

As lanterns guide us through the night,
In every step, we find the light.
With faith as compass, love our shield,
Towards sacred space, our souls are healed.

In whispers soft, the promise clear,
A sacred abode, forever near.
As rivers flow and winds do sing,
We move as one, embracing spring.

Each trial faced, a lesson learned,
In every heart, the fire burns.
The journey long, yet filled with grace,
Towards the sacred, we find our place.

In timeless bonds, our spirits soar,
In love's embrace, forevermore.
With every breath, the path unfolds,
A journey blessed, the truth beholds.

Harmony in the Rising Light

In the dawn's warm embrace, we find,
A whisper of hope in the gentle breeze.
The light of His love, ever kind,
Guides our hearts to a tranquil ease.

Birds sing hymns of joy and grace,
As shadows of night begin to fade.
In this sacred, holy space,
His presence forever shall be laid.

The sun breaks forth, painting the sky,
Each hue a promise of brighter days.
In the moments we feel small, shy,
His glory shines in myriad ways.

With every beat, the world aligns,
In unity we rise and stand tall.
His wisdom flows in pure designs,
In the silence, we hear His call.

Together, we walk hand in hand,
In harmony, our spirits soar.
Bound by faith, we take our stand,
In the light, we are forevermore.

Renewal in His Presence

In the stillness of the evening glow,
Hope blooms like flowers in spring's embrace.
With every breath, His blessings flow,
Washing over us, a sacred grace.

He mends the broken, heals the heart,
In His love, we find our strength renewed.
From shattered dreams, we can restart,
Awakening the joy once subdued.

Each moment cherished, a gift divine,
In the fabric of life, we weave our song.
Together, in unity, we shine,
In His presence, we always belong.

With open hearts, we seek His light,
Guided by faith through darkness and doubt.
In every struggle, He ignites,
A flicker of hope that will not go out.

As seasons change and shadows fall,
Our spirits rise, reborn and free.
In love's embrace, we stand tall,
Renewed in His grace, eternally.

A Symphony of the Soul

In the quiet moments, whispers play,
A melody born from heaven's grace.
Each heartbeat echoes in rhythmic sway,
A symphony that time cannot erase.

Voices lifted in prayers so sweet,
Harmonies woven through trials and tears.
In His presence, our souls compete,
Creating music that calms our fears.

With every note, a memory shines,
Of love that binds and truths that last.
Together, we dance on sacred lines,
In the chorus of all our past.

The grandeur of faith, a soaring song,
In the struggle, we find our refrain.
As one, we gather, together, strong,
In the symphony, we break every chain.

So let us sing of joy and peace,
In every heart, let His music flow.
With gratitude, may our praises increase,
In the symphony of love we know.

Between Earth and Heaven

In the silence where shadows dwell,
We seek the path that leads us higher.
With humble hearts, we know Him well,
Inspired by faith, ignited, aflame with fire.

Caught between the world we see,
And the promise of what lies ahead.
We yearn for His truth to set us free,
Guided by love that always spreads.

In moments of doubt, we find our way,
With every prayer, our spirits rise.
Between earth and heaven, night and day,
His wisdom shines, a guiding prize.

Together we wander this sacred ground,
With grace, we trust in the unseen.
In His embrace, our hearts are found,
A bridge that connects all that has been.

So let us walk in faith each day,
Between the realms, where dreams unfold.
In His light, we'll find the way,
Between earth and heaven, we are bold.

Reaching for the Celestial

With eyes lifted high to the skies,
We search for the stars where the holy lies.
In whispers of prayer, our spirits take flight,
Guided by faith in the glow of the night.

Each tear we've shed finds grace in the air,
In moments of silence, our hearts lay bare.
We seek the divine in the depths of our soul,
Embracing the truth that can make us whole.

The cosmos sings softly, a mystical tune,
In shadows and light we are cradled, as one.
With every step forward, we tread on the path,
Of love and compassion, escaping the wrath.

In unity's bond, we transcend the strife,
A tapestry woven of faith and of life.
Our hands reach together, an offering bright,
To the heavens above, bathing all in their light.

So let us ascend with our spirits aligned,
In the quest for the sacred, forever entwined.
For in reaching above, we shall find our way,
To the celestial embrace that will never decay.

The Light Renewed within

In silence we gather, hearts open wide,
Yearning for warmth that the soul cannot hide.
A flicker ignites in the depths of the dark,
With whispers of hope, we reclaim the spark.

The dawn breaks anew with a promise so clear,
Inviting the faithful to draw ever near.
In echoes of joy, our spirits resound,
As the light within us is lovingly found.

With each gentle heartbeat, we find our own way,
Through shadows of doubt, in the light of the day.
In the garden of mercy, our hearts bloom and thrive,
Awakening wisdom, we truly arrive.

The flame shines brighter as we gather around,
In each other's presence, pure grace can be found.
Forgive all our trespasses, and let love abide,
For the light once ignited can never subside.

We'll walk hand in hand, through trials and more,
In moments of faith, our spirits will soar.
For the light anew flows from within our soul,
A beacon of love that makes us all whole.

Climbing the Ladder to Heaven

With each upward step, we ardently climb,
To the heights of our spirits, transcending all time.
With courage as armor, our hearts beat as one,
Through valleys of shadows, towards the bright sun.

The rungs made of kindness, the strings of our grace,
Elevate our souls in this sacred embrace.
In unity's power, we rise above fear,
Bound by the promise that love will draw near.

Each challenge we face, a lesson designed,
To strengthen our will and connect heart and mind.
And as we ascend, the air thick with prayer,
We summon the strength found in love's gentle care.

With faith as our guide, we reach to the sky,
In the hands of the Divine, our spirits will fly.
Though the summit seems distant, we trust in the way,
That leads us to heaven at the close of the day.

So let us keep climbing, with hearts full of light,
Forming a chorus of hope in the night.
For in every ascent, we discover our worth,
Climbing the ladder that leads to new birth.

Embracing the Holy Wind

In the canopy high, where the faithful reside,
The holy wind whispers, an angelic guide.
It carries our prayers on its gentle breath,
Soothing our sorrows, defeating all death.

As leaves sway and dance in the sacred air,
We open our hearts, letting peace linger there.
In echoes of nature, the Spirit unfolds,
A story of love in the canvas it holds.

With each gust of hope, we are swept away,
Finding strength in surrender, come what may.
In the harmony woven through every refrain,
The holy wind stirs us, breaking each chain.

In moments of stillness, we hear the call clear,
To embrace the divine, casting aside fear.
The breath of creation, our hearts intertwined,
In the sacred connection, all souls are aligned.

So let us be open to what life will bring,
As we labor with love, our hearts taking wing.
In the embrace of the wind, we find solace and rest,
Awakening love in this journey, our quest.

Blossoming in His Love

In gardens rich with grace, we stand,
His gentle whispers, guiding hand.
Each flower blooms, a sacred sign,
In love divine, our hearts align.

The rays of hope, like sunlit streams,
Awake our souls, ignite our dreams.
With every petal, joy unfolds,
In every breath, His love upholds.

Through trials faced and joys we share,
In faith we walk, in holy prayer.
Through shadows cast, we find our way,
In love's embrace, we choose to stay.

Our roots entwined in humble ground,
In silence deep, His voice resound.
With every challenge, He bestows,
The strength to rise, His love still grows.

So let us flourish, sweet and free,
In His embrace, eternally.
For in His love, our spirits soar,
Forever cherished, evermore.

Lifting Shadows

When shadows fall and doubts arise,
We lift our gaze to endless skies.
With hearts united, we find light,
In faith, we turn the dark to bright.

Each prayer an echo, strong and clear,
A voice of hope, dispelling fear.
His grace, a lamp to guide our way,
In love's sweet arms, we choose to stay.

With voices raised, we sing His praise,
Through stormy nights and endless days.
In every teardrop, hope reflects,
A promise kept, in Him, we rest.

Through trials faced and battles fought,
With faith unspoken, lessons taught.
His presence near, a sacred shield,
In unity, our hearts are healed.

So let us lift the shadows high,
To dance upon the clouds of sky.
In gratitude, our spirits sing,
Awake in love, His grace we bring.

Between the Gauntlet and Glory

In valleys low where shadows creep,
A sacred promise we shall keep.
Between the trials and the fight,
His guiding hand brings hope and light.

We walk the path of weary souls,
With every heartbeat, faith consoles.
Mountains high and valleys deep,
In His embrace, our hearts shall leap.

With strength renewed, we face the race,
Between the strife and warm embrace.
His love, a beacon shining bright,
In darkest hours, the gift of sight.

Through gauntlets set, our spirits soar,
In every moment, we restore.
With arms outstretched, we seek His face,
In glory found, we claim our place.

So carry forth this truth we hold,
In every story, love unfold.
For in His name, we rise above,
Between the gauntlet and His love.

Cliffs of Faith

On cliffs of faith, we stand so tall,
In reverence, we heed His call.
With steadfast hearts, we take our stand,
In every step, we trust His hand.

Through storms that rage and winds that blow,
In faith's embrace, we find the flow.
With courage strong, we climb each height,
In valleys low, His love shines bright.

Though shadows lurk and doubts arise,
We lift our gaze to endless skies.
In every heartache, we find grace,
In every struggle, a sacred space.

So here we gather, bold and free,
With open hearts, our spirits see.
On cliffs of faith, we claim our place,
In Him we trust, our hopes embrace.

Together strong, we face the climb,
In Faith's embrace, we conquer time.
With every heartbeat, we shall sing,
On cliffs of faith, our praises ring.

The Path of Divine Awakening

In silence we tread, hearts aligned,
With whispers of grace, all intertwined.
Each step a reflection, a sacred intent,
Guided by light, through the heavens we went.

The shadows of doubt begin to recede,
As faith takes root, a blossoming seed.
In prayerful whispers, our spirits ignite,
Cradled in love, we embrace the light.

The path may be winding, yet gently it leads,
To the depths of our souls, where divinity feeds.
With hope as our compass, we venture anew,
Awakened to life, our spirits break through.

A journey of heart, an unfolding grace,
In the mirror of truth, see the sacred face.
Together we walk, hand in hand as we rise,
In the fullness of love, we become the wise.

So let us rejoice, in unity's song,
With every beat echoing, we all belong.
For on this path, we collectively find,
The divine in the heart, forever enshrined.

To the Peaks of Holy Joy

We climb the high mountains, where spirits soar,
In search of the treasures that grace can restore.
With faith as our guide, we face every test,
Embracing the journey, in love we find rest.

The air is more vibrant, each breath pure delight,
As hearts open wide to the divine light.
With laughter and hope, we dance in the skies,
United in joy, where happiness lies.

In the valleys of trials, we gather our strength,
With each step forward, we travel the length.
For in every struggle, the light will appear,
As grace weaves its magic, dissolving all fear.

A chorus of angels surrounds us each day,
In the moments of doubt, they guide us to pray.
Unfolding in harmony, our spirits renew,
In the peaks of holy joy, our hearts are made true.

So let us ascend, hand in hand through the trials,
With faith as our beacon, we embrace the miles.
For together we rise, in joy we transcend,
To the heights of His love, where our spirits ascend.

Embracing the Dawn of Redemption

In the hush of the morning, redemption awakes,
As shadows dissolve, the heart gently shakes.
With hands open wide, we welcome the light,
Embracing the dawn, the day conquers night.

Each breath a confession, a moment to heal,
In the sanctum of love, our truths we reveal.
Forgiveness like raindrops, washes all pain,
Renewed in His mercy, we rise once again.

The dawn paints the skies with colors of grace,
In the warmth of His love, we each find our place.
With hope in our hearts, we echo His song,
For in this redemption, we all do belong.

Beneath the vast heavens, we stand hand in hand,
Embracing the dawn, a united band.
For in every sunrise, a promise we find,
That love conquers all, uniting mankind.

So let every moment proclaim our rebirth,
In the depths of our souls, let us honor our worth.
For in each new dawn, redemption takes flight,
Guiding our spirits towards divine light.

Dancing in Sacred Radiance

In the circle of life, we gather as one,
Hearts beating in rhythm, our journey begun.
With hands raised in praise, we dance with delight,
In the sacred radiance, our spirits take flight.

Each twirl is a blessing, each step a refrain,
Celebrating love in both joy and in pain.
The music of grace weaves through every soul,
Binding us together, making us whole.

As stars shine above, guiding all of our ways,
We bask in their glow, through the night and the days.
With every heartbeat, we echo His love,
In this dance of devotion, we rise like a dove.

In the rhythm of life, we find pure release,
In the grace of the moment, our hearts find their peace.
With laughter and tears, we celebrate all,
In the sacred radiance, we answer the call.

So let us rejoice in this dance of the divine,
With every leap forward, our spirits align.
For in the sacred dance, our souls are set free,
In the beauty of love, we become what we see.

Unveiling the Sacred

In the stillness of the dawn,
Whispers of the holy speak,
Veils are lifted, truths shared,
A glimpse of what we seek.

Beneath the arching heavens wide,
The earth and spirit blend,
With every breath, the sacred tide,
Unites the heart to mend.

Ancient paths of wisdom call,
Guiding souls in need,
In humility, we stand tall,
From the seeds of love, we feed.

In the quiet, faith takes flight,
As light through shadows flows,
In each heart, a beacon bright,
The sacred presence glows.

Together we shall rise above,
On wings of grace we soar,
Finding peace in endless love,
Unveiling evermore.

In the Light of His Embrace

In the shadows faint and gray,
His light begins to break,
A gentle warmth, a guiding ray,
In every choice we make.

Hands uplifted, voices clear,
We come to seek His face,
In the laughter, in the tear,
We find our resting place.

Each moment, sacred, pure,
Wrapped in His embrace,
With faith, our hearts endure,
In love, we find our grace.

Through trials faced, together strong,
We walk the path of trust,
In His presence, we belong,
Faithful to the dust.

Anointed by His everlasting light,
We rise to meet the dawn,
In the depth of darkest night,
His love will lead us on.

Heart's Yearning

In the depth of silence, sighs,
A yearning fills the air,
Longing for the sacred ties,
To feel His presence there.

Each moment speaks of hope,
A tender prayer we weave,
In the shadows, we elope,
In faith, we shall believe.

Searching through the pages old,
Wisdom softly glows,
A journey brave and boldly told,
Where every heart still grows.

With every heartbeat, a whisper,
Echoes through the night,
In this dance, our spirit crisper,
In gratitude's sweet light.

Yearning hearts, we gather near,
In communion, souls are one,
Finding solace, casting fear,
Until our race is run.

Rebirth in Divine Love

From ashes rise, a soul reborn,
In love's embrace, a new dawn's sworn.
With open arms, the heart receives,
A sacred promise, one believes.

Through trials faced, in shadows cast,
Divine love whispers, holding fast.
In every tear, a lesson shown,
Through pain, the seeds of grace have grown.

The light within ignites the way,
Guiding us through both night and day.
In every heartbeat, each breath we take,
Rebirth unfolds, as fears forsake.

With faith as anchor, hope as guide,
Together we walk, side by side.
In every moment, love's song to sing,
Rebirth in divine, our souls take wing.

So let us cherish every hour,
The bond we share, a sacred flower.
In love's embrace, forever free,
Rebirth in divine love, you and me.

Ascension of the Spirit

In whispers soft, the Spirit calls,
To rise above these earthly thralls.
With wings of faith, we soar on high,
Embracing grace beneath the sky.

Through trials fierce, and shadows cast,
The heart finds strength within the vast.
With every breath, in truth we tread,
In love divine, our souls are fed.

A sacred light, it guides our way,
Through night and storm, to hope's bright day.
In unity our voices blend,
In sacred songs, our spirits mend.

The pinnacle, where peace resides,
In joy's embrace, the heart abides.
With outstretched arms, we welcome grace,
In harmony, we find our place.

Ascend, oh soul, to realms above,
In every heartbeat, know His love.
As stars align in cosmic dance,
In this communion, find your chance.

From Shadow to Light

From shadowed paths, we make our soar,
To find the light, the heart's great core.
The dawn awakens, bright and clear,
In every moment, His voice we hear.

Beneath the weight of doubt and fear,
The guiding hand is always near.
In whispered prayers, our hopes ignite,
Transcending dark, we walk to light.

With every step, the past shall fade,
In faith, the burdens gently laid.
A radiant truth begins to shine,
In love's embrace, our souls entwine.

Through valleys deep, and mountain high,
In every challenge, we learn to fly.
With courage bold, the spirit leaps,
In every wound, His healing keeps.

From shadow's veil to glory bright,
We rise as one, transformed by light.
In unity, our voices sing,
Praise to the dawn, and life it brings.

In the Embrace of Dawn

As dawn awakens, softly bright,
Hope fills the heart, dispelling night.
In gentle whispers, love's decree,
Awaits the spirit, wild and free.

The morn unfolds with tender care,
In every breath, the spirit's prayer.
With open hands, we seek to find,
The sacred peace that binds all kind.

In every petal, grace displays,
The beauty found in quiet praise.
Through trials, storms, and endless fight,
We find our strength, in love's pure light.

Rising sun, you guide our way,
Transform our hearts, and lead to stay.
In trust, we walk where shadows roam,
In faith, we claim our spirit's home.

In the embrace of dawn, we rise,
With grateful hearts, we touch the skies.
In unity, our spirits blend,
A sacred bond that never ends.

Divine Lifting

In moments still, we hear the grace,
That lifts the soul to heaven's space.
With every prayer, we seek the climb,
In joyous echoes, through all time.

The breath of life, a sacred song,
In love's embrace, we all belong.
With open hearts, we rise anew,
In divine lifting, He guides us through.

With eyes uplifted, we shall see,
The beauty found in harmony.
In every challenge, hope ignites,
Through darkest nights, we chase the lights.

In sacred circles, our spirits fuse,
In every choice, our love we choose.
With every step, the path unfolds,
In trust and faith, the heart beholds.

As mountains bow and oceans part,
In divine lifting, we share one heart.
In chorus strong, we sing our tune,
United in dance, beneath the moon.

A Soul's Flight towards Eternity

In the stillness of the night,
A whisper calls the heart to rise,
Through the veils of time and light,
The soul begins its endless skies.

Above the clouds, beyond the stars,
Each step a dance with sacred grace,
Unbinding chains, erasing scars,
Embracing love in every space.

In the glow of the celestial,
The spirit finds its wings anew,
Transcending bounds, so ethereal,
Awash in colors bold and true.

With every breath, pure peace descends,
In harmony with the divine,
A journey where the heart transcends,
The soul awakens, bright, and fine.

Each star a hope, a sacred dream,
Guiding us through the endless night,
In love's embrace, forever gleam,
A beacon in the endless flight.

Steps Toward Heaven

With every step, I feel the grace,
Guiding me along the way,
Footprints soft in sacred space,
In love, I choose to stay.

Each stone a blessing, each turn a prayer,
A journey to the skies,
In the burden, I find care,
In the waiting, faith will rise.

With open heart and lifted eye,
I walk on paths divine,
In His presence, I rely,
For every step is mine.

Though the road may twist and bend,
I trust in what I feel,
With every twist, His love ascends,
In Him, my heart is healed.

Toward the heavens, I will climb,
With strength to carry on,
In every breath, His love, sublime,
Will guide me 'til I'm home.

Transcendence of the Heart

In the stillness, the soul does soar,
Touching realms where love is more.
Hearts united, spirits free,
In the light of unity.

Whispers echo through the night,
Guided by a sacred light.
Beneath the stars, we find our way,
In faith's embrace, we choose to stay.

Mountains crumble, waters flow,
Life's great journey will bestow.
With each step, the heart does call,
Transcendence waits beyond the fall.

Breathe in mercy, exhale grace,
In every heart, a sacred space.
Together, in prayer, let spirit blend,
Love's pure promise has no end.

So let us rise, no fear defy,
In truth, we live, awake, and high.
For in the silence, we each shall see,
The transcendence of unity.

The Song of the Morning Star

Awake, arise, the dawn is bright,
The morning star ignites the night.
With every ray, the shadows flee,
A song of hope, serene and free.

Whispers soft as the breeze do sing,
Of love renewed, the joy we bring.
Each heart a vessel, pure and true,
Guided by the light anew.

In fields of gold, the flowers bloom,
A testament to love's sweet tune.
With every chord, let voices blend,
The song of life, it has no end.

In moments still, we find the grace,
Of tender mercy, heart's embrace.
Through trials faced, we stand as one,
In the warmth of the rising sun.

So let us dance, the world to fill,
With joy and peace, and spirit's will.
For in each note, our lives inspire,
The song of hope, the morning fire.

Faithful Rise

In valleys low, the faithful tread,
With heavy hearts and daily bread.
Yet in the dusk, a light will gleam,
For in the dark, we hold our dream.

Each prayer a step, each tear a seed,
In love's embrace, we find the creed.
Together we rise, hand in hand,
In unity the spirit stands.

With every dawn, a chance to grow,
The light of faith begins to flow.
Through storms we walk, our heads held high,
For in the struggle, we learn to fly.

In doubt's despair, the heart will sing,
The song of hope that faith can bring.
With open hearts, we shall ignite,
A fire within, our souls take flight.

So let us rise, with strength anew,
In love's embrace, there's much to do.
With every breath, we weave our fate,
In faithful rise, we celebrate.

Cherishing the Radiance of Hope

In the dawn of a brand new day,
Hope stirs within the gentle dawn,
Like flowers waking from the gray,
To greet the light, a new world born.

With every heartbeat, faith ignites,
A spark that shines through trials faced,
In darkest hours, the spirit fights,
For love endures, and dreams are traced.

In the tapestry of the skies,
Each thread a promise woven tight,
We glimpse the truth beyond the lies,
As shadows yield to radiant light.

Embracing grace in times of fear,
We walk with courage in our stride,
With each small step, the path grows clear,
As hope illuminates our guide.

Let not despair our hearts confine,
For in the soul, a fire glows,
With every prayer, a love divine,
In unity, our spirit flows.

Treading the Path of Sacred Dreams

Step gently on this hallowed ground,
Where every whisper speaks of grace,
In every heartbeat, love is found,
As souls entwine, we find our place.

With faith, we tread this sacred road,
Each moment blooms with endless light,
In acts of kindness, love bestowed,
We share our burdens, hearts unite.

The mountains high, the valleys low,
A journey carved by hope and tears,
With every challenge, we shall grow,
In trust, we cast away our fears.

Let fervent prayers rise like the dawn,
Each word a thread that binds us close,
As we pursue the dreams foregone,
With courage found in love's sweet prose.

In every heartbeat, echoes blend,
A chorus sung in unity,
On this path where dreams ascend,
We walk with grace, eternally.

When the Spirit Awakens

In the silence, whispers flow,
A stirring deep within the soul,
When the spirit wakes to know,
Its purpose, truth, and sacred whole.

Eyes opened wide, the heart expands,
To embrace the light, the love so near,
With gentle strength, the spirit stands,
In grace, it conquers doubt and fear.

In every moment, blessings bloom,
As faith ignites a wondrous flame,
Through shadows, music drowns the gloom,
The spirit calls, a sacred name.

Beneath the stars, we rise anew,
With every breath, a promise made,
As love flows forth, so pure and true,
In unity, the world remade.

So let the spirit soar and sing,
Awakened hearts in harmony,
Embrace the joy that love can bring,
In every soul, divinity.

Awakening to the Divine Light

In silence whispered prayers arise,
Hearts open wide beneath the skies.
A gentle warmth begins to glow,
Awakening dreams that softly flow.

With hands uplifted, we seek the grace,
Finding solace in the sacred space.
Eyes closed, we breathe in love's sweet sound,
In the still, our spirits rebound.

The world fades as we close our eyes,
Underneath the vast, endless skies.
In unity, we cast away fear,
Awakening light, drawing it near.

Each moment cherished, each heartbeat divine,
We shine together as stars align.
A sacred dance through the ebb and flow,
In the arms of the One, we shall grow.

With faith as our compass, we walk as one,
Guided by light, our journey's begun.
Awakening whispers, a celestial song,
In this holy embrace, we belong.

Ascending through Faith's Embrace

In shadows deep, we find our way,
With faith as anchor, come what may.
Each step we take, a prayer in hand,
In unison, together we stand.

Through trials faced, we rise anew,
In love's embrace, we are made true.
Eyes lifted to the heavens above,
Absorbing light, the essence of love.

The path unfolds, a sacred trail,
With courage strong, we will not fail.
Holding tightly to hope's sweet song,
In faith's embrace, we find where we belong.

The spirit soars with each gentle breath,
Transcending beyond the veil of death.
In unity, our hearts ignite,
Ascending ever towards the light.

As dawn breaks forth, shadows take flight,
We bask in the warmth of radiant light.
Each journey begins within the heart,
United in purpose, never apart.

The Dawn of Sacred Hope

As dawn awakens, a promise unfolds,
Whispers of love in the stories told.
With each sunrise, new strength appears,
Washing away all sorrows and fears.

In the garden of faith, seeds are sown,
Through trials and tears, our spirits have grown.
Hope shines brightly, a beacon of grace,
Illuminating paths that we embrace.

In the stillness, we find our song,
Together in harmony, where we belong.
Each note a prayer, a sacred release,
In the dawn of hope, we find our peace.

Clouds may gather, storms may brew,
Yet in our hearts, hope stays true.
For after the night, the dawn shall rise,
Painting colors across the skies.

With open arms, we welcome the light,
Casting away the shadows of night.
In unity, a promise we shape,
As we stand together, in hope's great escape.

Heavens Lift Me Higher

When burdens weigh and spirits wane,
I look to the heavens, free from pain.
With faith like wings, I soar above,
Embraced by the warmth of endless love.

In still reflection, I hear the call,
A voice that lifts, embracing all.
Through trials faced, I rise and stand,
In the heart of grace, I understand.

Each moment precious, a gift divine,
As joy cascades like sweetened wine.
With every heartbeat, closer drawn,
To the whispering light of the dawn.

In sacred silence, I find my peace,
A gentle promise that will not cease.
With open heart, I seek to climb,
For heaven's touch transcends all time.

As clouds disperse, I feel the sun,
A radiant glow, I am now one.
In love's embrace, I rise and fly,
With heavens behind me, I aim for the sky.

In the Silence of Dawn

In the hush of dawn's gentle breath,
Whispers of grace fill the air.
The world awakens from night's soft death,
Hope rises with the day's first glare.

Birds sing hymns to the loving light,
Each note a prayer, pure and clear.
Stars fade slowly, taking flight,
In the presence of the Divine near.

With every heartbeat, spirits soar,
The sun paints skies with hues divine.
In this moment, we seek and explore,
The promise of love, eternally mine.

Softly we gather, hearts entwined,
In the silence, peace abounds.
Finding strength in what we find,
In the dawn, the sacred resounds.

Blessed are those who hear the call,
In the light of a new-born day.
United, we rise, never to fall,
In the silence of dawn, we pray.

Embracing the Sacred Journey

With each step upon this path,
We walk the way of love and grace.
In trials faced, we find our wrath,
Yet know we're held in His embrace.

Mountains loom but hearts are brave,
Guided by a light so bright.
Through every storm, the soul will save,
In shadows cast, we seek the light.

Each moment, a lesson, a chance to grow,
In joy and sorrow, we weave our part.
Embracing the journey, letting love flow,
Trusting the plan penned in our heart.

As rivers twist, so does our fate,
The sacred journey, a dance divine.
With faith as our compass, we navigate,
Together in spirit, our souls align.

Let gratitude blossom like flowers in spring,
For every struggle builds our song.
In unity, our praises we bring,
Embracing the journey, where we belong.

The Radiance of Tomorrow

In the dawn of hope, dreams awaken,
Each ray a promise, bright and new.
The past, though heavy, will not be shaken,
For light will guide us, pure and true.

Voices rise in a sacred chorus,
Melodies weave through the breeze.
Hearts open wide, love's powerful force,
In the radiance, burdens cease.

Visions of peace, we hold them dear,
With every prayer, our spirits ignite.
As we gather, dispelling fear,
Together we shine, a beacon of light.

Tomorrow whispers with gentle grace,
A tapestry rich with dreams fulfilled.
In love's embrace, we find our place,
Hearts intertwined, our hopes distilled.

Let us rise, united and free,
In faith, we journey toward the sun.
The radiance of tomorrow we see,
In love's truth, we are forever one.

Heart's Dance in the Light

In the warmth of the sun's embrace,
Our hearts awaken to the day.
With each beat, we find our grace,
In the light, we learn to sway.

Like petals flutter in the breeze,
Our spirits twirl in joyous song.
In harmony, we find our ease,
Together, we are where we belong.

With hands raised high and eyes closed tight,
We offer thanks for every breath.
In the radiance of love's bright light,
We dance through life, defying death.

Each moment shared, a bond so sweet,
In the melody of grace, we unite.
With every rhythm, our souls entreat,
In the heart's dance, we find our light.

Let sorrow fade, let joy take flight,
As we embrace the sacred night.
In the circle of love, life takes its height,
Our heart's dance forever bright.

Surfing on Waves of Mercy

In the depth of night, grace flows,
Gentle whispers of love bestow,
With every tide, I rise and fall,
In mercy's arms, I hear the call.

Each wave a blessing, pure and bright,
Guiding me through darkest plight,
The ocean vast, my spirit sails,
On currents of hope where faith prevails.

The sun reflects on azure seas,
A sacred song that sets me free,
With every splash, my soul ignites,
In mercy's grace, my heart delights.

Riding high on fervent prayer,
A journey found in sacred care,
With each swell, I trust and strive,
On waves of mercy, I feel alive.

So let the waters cleanse my way,
Each droplet speaks of a new day,
In surfing, I find my divine,
On waves of mercy, love will shine.

Light Breaking through the Tempest

When storms arise and shadows creep,
My heart clings tight, my soul to keep,
Yet through the thunder, hope appears,
A beacon bright that calms my fears.

The tempest rages, fierce and loud,
But faith stands firm, a steadfast crowd,
In darkness, light begins to break,
A guiding star, my spirit wakes.

Each raindrop falls, a whispered prayer,
In every trial, Your love I share,
The skies will clear, the sun will rise,
With every tear, Your grace supplies.

Through shifting winds, I will not sway,
For in Your arms, I find my way,
The storm may howl, but I am still,
With light Divine, my heart to fill.

So let the waves crash all around,
In faith and love, my hope is found,
For light shall break, and I will sing,
Of joy and peace, my offering.

The Sacred Symphony of Ascendancy

In the stillness, I hear the call,
A symphony that breaks the fall,
Each note a step towards the sky,
In harmony, my soul will fly.

With every chord, the heart will rise,
A melody that serves the wise,
In sacred space, the music flows,
Awakening all that love knows.

In whispered prayers, the voices blend,
In unity, on You I depend,
The sacred sound, a guiding light,
In this ascent, my spirit's flight.

Through trials faced and burdens borne,
The symphony of hope is born,
With every beat, I journey far,
In faith's embrace, You're my North Star.

As I ascend, I shed my fear,
In sacred song, I hold You near,
The symphony leads me to grace,
In every note, I find Your face.

Ethereal Echoes of the Heart

In silence deep, I hear You speak,
The echoes soft, the wisdom meek,
In every breath, the sacred art,
The music flows from Your sweet heart.

With gentle whispers, hopes arise,
In beauty found, beneath the skies,
Through trials faced with steadfast grace,
The echoes guide, I find my place.

Each moment shines, eternity,
In Your embrace, I am set free,
The rhythms of love beat within,
A dance divine where life begins.

In timeless space, connections grow,
The heart's soft call, the light will show,
In every tear, a joy is found,
In echoes pure, Your love surrounds.

So let me walk this path of light,
In ethereal love, my spirit's flight,
With every echo, truth will start,
In the sacred song, You fill my heart.

The Journey of the Heart

Upon the path of faith we tread,
Guided by whispers of love unsaid.
With each step, a promise to keep,
In the arms of grace, our souls leap.

Trials may come, like shadows at night,
Yet within us, a flicker of light.
Through valleys deep and mountains high,
Our spirits soar, learning to fly.

In stillness found, the heart does hear,
A gentle voice that calms all fear.
With hope as our compass, we navigate,
Ever closer to the divine gate.

Oh, journey long, with lessons in tow,
Each heartbeat a story, a chance to grow.
With faith as our vessel, we sail the sea,
In the arms of the Father, forever free.

Each turn of the heart, a sacred embrace,
Finding divinity woven in grace.
In unity bound, we rise above,
Together we journey, bound by love.

Grace's New Day

A dawn breaks soft, grace paints the sky,
With colors of hope, inviting the sigh.
Each moment a gift, wrapped in divine,
A chance to renew, a promise to shine.

The world awakens with gentle light,
Wings of the spirit take joyful flight.
In every heartbeat, a chance to see,
The beauty of life, in simplicity.

With eyes of love, the soul will find,
A pathway etched, in the heart and mind.
The whispers of grace guide our way,
As we step boldly into the day.

Let laughter ring, let kindness flow,
In each tiny act, let our true selves show.
The blessings abound, in each little deed,
In the tapestry woven, in love, we lead.

So greet the morning, with open hands,
For grace's new day, forever stands.
With faith as our anchor, we shall proceed,
In a world adorned with hope's pure seed.

Emerging from the Depths

From shadows deep, the soul ascends,
In waters dark, the spirit mends.
A call to rise, to breathe anew,
Embraced by light, our hearts break through.

Each struggle faced, a mountain climbed,
Within the storm, the truth we find.
From ashes we rise, reborn in flame,
With every wound, we grow our name.

The depths may linger, but hope ignites,
In darkest hours, our faith invites.
With courage bold, we take each stride,
In the arms of mercy, we shall abide.

Gathering strength from trials past,
We seek the horizon, our shadows cast.
Emergence is sweet, a dance of grace,
In the heart's embrace, we find our place.

So let the light lead, let it shine bright,
Guiding our way through the longest night.
With love as our armor, we shall be whole,
Emerging from depths, renewing the soul.

Light's Gentle Touch

A whisper of dawn, the light breaks free,
Gilding the world in harmony.
With tender caress, it warms the soul,
In every heartbeat, we feel the whole.

Upon the hilltop, shadows retreat,
As light descends, a moment sweet.
In its embrace, we find our way,
Guided by love, come what may.

Each step a dance, with grace we glide,
In the glow of mercy, we abide.
The heart is opened, the spirit sings,
As joy unravels, on angel's wings.

Rest in the light, let worries cease,
In every flicker, find perfect peace.
With hands uplifted, we greet the new,
In the gentle touch, we are made true.

So let the light lead, with its warm rays,
Illuminating our winding ways.
A sacred journey, together we trust,
In light's gentle touch, our hearts adjust.

Whispers of Resurrection

In the hush of dawn's embrace,
Life stirs from eternal sleep.
Hope rises in gentle grace,
From shadows, dreams awaken deep.

With every heartbeat, a promise new,
The soul's journey begins once more.
Through trials faced, we blossom true,
In faith's embrace, we are restored.

Grace flows like a river wide,
Washing away the pain of yore.
In love's warmth, we shall abide,
And find peace on the sacred shore.

Each tear sown becomes a seed,
In the garden of the heart's domain.
From ashes rise, the spirit freed,
In divine light, we break the chain.

Whispers call through the silent night,
Guiding the lost towards the day.
In every struggle, discover light,
Resurrection's song paved the way.

Unfurling into Grace

Soft petals unfold in prayer,
Reaching for the sun above.
In each moment, grace laid bare,
Embracing all with tender love.

The journey bends, yet never breaks,
With every step, the spirit grows.
In trials faced, the heart awakes,
Unfurling truth, as wisdom flows.

Through valleys low, past mountains high,
The soul finds wings to soar anew.
In whispers of the wind, we fly,
To find the light in skies so blue.

Let burdens lift like autumn leaves,
As faith ignites the path ahead.
The heart believes what love conceives,
In grace, our souls are gently led.

With every heartbeat, hope remains,
In the dance of life, we engage.
Unfurling softly through our pains,
We find our place upon the stage.

The Divine Symphony

Notes of love echo through time,
A symphony composed in grace.
Each heartbeat rings, a sacred rhyme,
In harmony, we find our place.

Voices rise, a celestial choir,
Singing praises to the skies.
In every heart, a burning fire,
Awakening the spirit's ties.

Resonance of the soul's delight,
In rhythm, lives entwined in song.
Guided by the celestial light,
To the heart's melody, we belong.

Chords of mercy weave the air,
Binding us in love's embrace.
Through trials, yet we find we care,
In this divine and sacred space.

As the symphony plays on,
Grace unfolds in every note.
In unity, we are drawn,
To the melody of hope we wrote.

To Heights Unseen

In silence whispers pull us higher,
To realms that dance beyond our sight.
Awakening the hidden fire,
In shadows born, we find the light.

Mountains rise, beneath feet they shake,
With every step, ascension's call.
Through trials faced, the heart won't break,
In faith, we rise, we shall not fall.

Each soul a star in night's expanse,
Guided by the love within.
In sacred journeys, we enhance,
The beauty where our dreams begin.

The winds of change embrace our hearts,
Lifting us to heights unseen.
With every breath, new life imparts,
In unity, our spirits glean.

As dawn reveals the path ahead,
We follow where the heart does lead.
In faith's embrace, we shall be fed,
To heights unseen, our souls are freed.

In the Shelter of Faith

In the stillness, He surrounds,
With whispers soft, His love abounds.
A refuge found where hearts align,
In trust we stand, in faith divine.

The storms may rage, yet here we dwell,
In sacred peace, all fears dispel.
His hand a shield, His heart a guide,
With every breath, we walk beside.

Through trials vast, our spirits rise,
In darkest nights, we seek His skies.
Each tear we shed, a seed of grace,
In every moment, we find His face.

Together bound in holy prayer,
Our voices lift, our burdens share.
In unity, we forge ahead,
With hope anew, by love we're led.

So let us trust, as shadows fade,
In faith's embrace, our souls are laid.
For evermore, we will not stray,
In shelter found, we humbly pray.

Gazing Upon the Infinite

Beneath the stars, our spirits soar,
In quiet awe, we seek once more.
The universe, a canvas vast,
In each small spark, the die is cast.

With every dawn, the sun anew,
A promise writ in golden hue.
We ponder depths both wide and high,
In every breath, we ask the why.

His presence dwells in cosmic grace,
In swirling worlds, we find our place.
Through galaxies, our hearts will roam,
In faith we stand, we're never alone.

The mysteries within us bloom,
A sacred song dispelling gloom.
Each moment here, a gift bestowed,
In love's embrace, our spirits glow.

So lift your eyes, and see the light,
In every shadow, hope ignites.
Together we will seek and find,
The infinite that stirs the mind.

The Climb of the Spirit

Upon the mountain, steep and high,
We seek the path where dreams can fly.
Each step a prayer, each breath a plea,
In struggle find our spirit free.

The rocks may bruise, the winds may howl,
Yet in His strength, we rise, we prowl.
With faith as guide, we face the test,
In toil and sweat, our souls are blessed.

Upward we strive, through doubts and fears,
In every heart, His love appears.
The summit calls, a promise bright,
With every rise, we gain new sight.

When shadows loom, don't lose your way,
For light will break a brand new day.
In perseverance, our spirits bind,
For in the climb, true peace we find.

So onward tread, through thick and thin,
With hearts aflame, let courage win.
For at the peak, we'll stand and see,
The grace that flows eternally.

The Light that Guides Us

Amid the darkness, shines a flame,
In silent whispers, calls His name.
A guiding star, through barren land,
In every step, we take His hand.

With open hearts, our souls ignite,
In hope's embrace, we find the light.
Each wound and scar, a lesson learned,
In trials faced, true wisdom earned.

The lantern glows, casting its hue,
In every shadow, He brings us through.
Together bound, we seek the way,
In unity, we rise and pray.

Through valleys low, and mountains steep,
In quiet moments, His love we keep.
With every turn, our spirits soar,
In trust we find, forevermore.

So let us walk with faith as guide,
Through every tempest, by His side.
In light's embrace, our hearts will sing,
For in His love, we find our wings.

Revelations of Joyful Ascent

In the stillness, praises rise,
Hearts united, souls in ties.
Mountains high, we strive to climb,
Joyful whispers, sacred rhyme.

With every step, faith intertwined,
Guided by grace, so divine.
Hope ignites the darkest night,
Basking in the holy light.

Voices join, a sweet refrain,
Echoes of our deep refrain.
In this dance, we find our way,
Trusting love, come what may.

The path unfolds, a vibrant hue,
Written in skies, a promise true.
With open hearts, we now ascend,
In joy we rise, with God, our friend.

Each revelation, a gift bestowed,
On the journey, love has flowed.
In the warmth of His embrace,
We find our home, our sacred space.

In the Light of Celestial Love

Bright stars twinkle, glimmers of grace,
In celestial realms, we seek our place.
Guided forth by a hand unseen,
Where love shines bright, and hearts are keen.

In the morning's golden glow,
Hope awakens, gentle flow.
Each heartbeat, a silent song,
In His presence, we belong.

Through valleys low, and mountains high,
In every tear, the Lord draws nigh.
Love's embrace will never fade,
In His arms, we're unafraid.

Radiant skies, a canvas wide,
With every shade, our hearts abide.
In this light, all burdens cease,
Through His love, we find our peace.

Now together, hand in hand,
Across the earth, we make our stand.
In the light of love's decree,
We rise above, forever free.

The Unfolding of the Spirit's Wings

In quiet whispers, wings take flight,
The spirit soars, embracing light.
Each feather sways to heaven's tune,
Beneath the stars, beneath the moon.

With every breath, the truth we find,
Hearts awakened, souls entwined.
Boundless grace, like rivers flow,
In the spirit's dance, we grow.

Through love's embrace, we learn to rise,
As hope ignites, the spirit flies.
Open skies invite the brave,
To embrace the love we crave.

In every trial, we will stand,
Together strong, hand in hand.
The wings of faith, they span so wide,
With joy as our eternal guide.

The journey blooms, we lift our gaze,
In this light, our hearts ablaze.
As the spirit's wings unfold,
We find our strength; we are consoled.

Awakening of the Soul

Beneath the stars, the silence sings,
Awakening the soul that clings.
To the gentle breeze of night,
A whisper calls, 'Come find your light.'

In shadows deep, we seek the flame,
The spark of love, a holy name.
Through trials faced, we rise anew,
In every challenge, faith shines through.

With every dawn, redemption's kiss,
In valleys low, we find pure bliss.
In humble hearts, the truth does dwell,
A sacred story, ours to tell.

The soul awakens, sweet and bold,
In love's embrace, our dreams unfold.
With open arms, we greet the day,
In unity, we find our way.

Through every storm, we hold the light,
In love's embrace, we conquer night.
Awakening to life's great whole,
Together, we uplift the soul.

The Spirit Soars in Light

In the hush of dawn's embrace,
The spirit lifts in grace,
Echoing the sacred call,
In unity, we rise, not fall.

Above the clouds, where angels sing,
Hope ignites, it's faith we bring,
With every step, the light does guide,
Through storms we walk, with hearts open wide.

In the stillness, whispers flow,
Warming souls like the sun's glow,
Each moment a blessing, pure and bright,
In truth, the spirit soars in light.

Joy awakens in our chest,
In every trial, we find rest,
With love's embrace, we find our way,
Through shadows turned to a brand new day.

Together we rise, hand in hand,
In faith's embrace, we take our stand,
For every heart that beats as one,
In the dance of spirit, we are spun.

Ascension of the Heart

Beneath the stars, a path unfolds,
In grace, the heart conquers bold,
With every breath, we transform,
In quiet stillness, love is born.

Through trials faced, we rise anew,
With faith as our anchor, ever true,
In twilight's glow, dreams take flight,
In the ascension of the heart's light.

Whispers of wisdom softly call,
In the depth, we learn to stand tall,
No fear shall dim the spirit's spark,
For in love's warmth, we ignite the dark.

Heavens open, blessings rain,
In every joy, a hint of pain,
Yet in the struggle, we find peace,
As the heart's ascent shall never cease.

With open arms, we greet the dawn,
In love's embrace, we are reborn,
Through every moment, grace imparts,
The sacred journey of the heart.

Glorious Beginnings in Faith

In the silence, a whisper flows,
In hearts uniting, hope still grows,
Each dawn a chance, a brand new day,
Guided by faith, we find our way.

Together we rise as the morning shines,
With joy and love, our spirit entwines,
In every moment, blessings shine bright,
Awakening dreams in divine light.

With open hearts, we seek the truth,
In the dance of wisdom, eternal youth,
With every prayer, the soul takes flight,
In glorious beginnings, we find our light.

Through trials faced, we learn and grow,
In faith's embrace, we let love flow,
Together we forge a path divine,
In union, our spirits brightly shine.

With gratitude, we lift our voice,
In every heartbeat, we rejoice,
For in this journey, we are one,
In glorious faith, our lives begun.

From Shadows, I Transcend

In shadows deep, where doubts reside,
A flicker of light, my hope's guide,
With every heartbeat, I reclaim,
The strength to rise, to fan the flame.

Through valleys low, my spirit learns,
In silent prayer, the heart yearns,
Each scar a story, woven bold,
In the tapestry of faith untold.

With courage fierce, I face the night,
In darkness, I find the inner light,
From brokenness, my soul ascends,
In the rebirth, the spirit mends.

With grace, I walk upon this earth,
In shadows turned to sacred mirth,
Awakening dreams once thought to end,
In the journey of life, I transcend.

Together, we rise, hand in hand,
In the unity of love, we stand,
Through every storm, the light shall send,
A promise of peace, from shadows, I transcend.

Journeying to the Sacred

In the quiet night, the stars do glow,
Footsteps lead soft, as whispers flow.
A path is drawn where shadows fade,
Hope illuminates the faithful trade.

With every step, the spirit sings,
Anointed grace, the soul it brings.
Each prayer a lantern, burning bright,
Guiding the heart through endless night.

Here in the stillness, peace is found,
In humble journeys, love's abound.
We walk the line of grace divine,
In sacred trust, our souls entwine.

Mountains high, valleys low,
Through trials faced, we learn to grow.
In every tear, a blessing sown,
In every trial, His love is known.

As dawn breaks forth, new light appears,
A promise held, dispelling fears.
We journey on, hearts open wide,
In the sacred space, He'll be our guide.

Horizon of Faith

Through valleys deep and skies of gray,
We seek the truth, the light of day.
Each dawn awakens hope anew,
The horizon calls, as dreams break through.

With every breath, a prayer we share,
In whispered trust, we find Him there.
The sun will rise on weary trails,
In unity, the spirit prevails.

The winds will carry our silent pleas,
In every rustle of the trees.
Faith is the thread that gently weaves,
The fabric of grace that never leaves.

When shadows darken the path we tread,
In hearts of stone, where angels led.
We'll rise above with voices strong,
In sacred hymns, we all belong.

The horizon stretches, vast and wide,
Together we walk, side by side.
With faith as anchor, love the guide,
In the light of truth, forever abide.

The Ascent of the Righteous

To lofty peaks, we lift our eyes,
In search of wisdom, truth, and ties.
Each step we take, a choice of grace,
In the ascent, we find our place.

The path is steep, but hearts are bold,
With every story, love unfolds.
In trials met, the spirit soars,
Through faith ignited, the heart implores.

Together bound, we climb the hill,
In gentle whispers, the heart is still.
The summit waits, a promise cheers,
In unity, we shed our fears.

With every triumph, shadows fade,
In love's embrace, each debt is paid.
We stand as one, the righteous true,
With arms outstretched, we start anew.

The view is vast from heights we gain,
In joy and peace, there's no more pain.
Together we'll tread, forever bright,
In the ascent, we find our light.

Emancipation of the Heart

In chains of doubt, the heart may ache,
Yet love's embrace, a bond to break.
With faith aflame, we seek release,
In holy silence, we find peace.

The soul unshackles, fears laid bare,
In gentle grace, we learn to care.
Through trials faced, we rise above,
In every moment, we find His love.

The spirit dances, free and wild,
In sacred joy, the heart, a child.
Each tear shed, a river flows,
Emancipated, the spirit grows.

With open arms, we greet the day,
In every heartbeat, a sacred ray.
The chains of past dissolve away,
In love's embrace, we choose to stay.

Together we wander, hearts alight,
In every shadow, we find the light.
Emancipation, the sweetest art,
In love we find the endless heart.

A Divine Ascendance

In stillness of the night we rise,
To seek the light beyond the skies.
Whispers of angels guide our way,
In sacred realms where spirits play.

With every heart that yearns to soar,
The love of God opens the door.
Embracing grace, we find our peace,
In harmony where all fears cease.

The stars above sing songs of old,
Of faith and hope in that which's told.
We climb the heights, our souls set free,
An endless dance of unity.

In each ascent, our burdens shed,
To walk with Him, our spirits fed.
We touch the divine and feel the flame,
In every heartbeat, we praise His name.

The way may twist, the path may bend,
Yet in His love, we find our mend.
Together, hand in hand we rise,
Toward the light that never dies.

The Sacred Journey Home

Upon a path to light divine,
We tread with faith, our hearts align.
Each step we take, a prayer released,
In gratitude, our souls find peace.

Through valleys deep and mountains high,
We seek the truth that cannot die.
The whispers of our spirit's call,
Remind us we are one with all.

We carry love through every storm,
In sacred trust, our hearts stay warm.
The journey long, yet filled with grace,
As we embrace the holy space.

In moments lost, we still believe,
Through every trial, we shall achieve.
With every breath, our purpose shines,
In unity, our spirit twines.

And when at last the road does yield,
We'll break the chains that once were sealed.
Back to the arms of love we roam,
In timeless light, we find our home.

Foundation of Light

In the dawn's embrace we find,
The whispers of the sacred mind.
A light that leads through shadowed night,
In every heart, the promise bright.

With faith as strong as mountain stone,
We build a world that feels like home.
Each moment blessed, a gift from above,
A testament to faith and love.

In unity, our spirits blend,
Creating joy that will not end.
Together, we stand hand in hand,
A living testament, a holy band.

As sunlight streams through every hour,
We bloom as one, a living flower.
In harmony, we walk this path,
Through trials met, we find the math.

The foundation laid upon His grace,
A sacred bond we all embrace.
In every heart, His light we hold,
A shining story yet untold.

Harmonizing with the Divine

In whispers soft, the soul ascends,
To realms where time and space transcends.
The melody of life we sing,
In harmony with everything.

In every breath, a sacred note,
The love of God, our hearts devote.
With gratitude, we rise and bow,
In every moment, here and now.

We dance with stars, we sing with trees,
In nature's arms, we find our ease.
The sacred rhythms guide our way,
In peace, our spirits long to stay.

With open hearts, we feel the flow,
The pulse of life, a gentle glow.
In unity, we find our song,
A chorus of love, ever strong.

As we attune to love's embrace,
We find our place in sacred space.
Together, let our voices chime,
In harmonizing with the divine.

The Dawning of Hope

In the quiet dawn, light breaks anew,
Whispers of promise fill the morning dew.
With hearts uplifted, we rise and sing,
For in this moment, hope takes wing.

Clouds of despair begin to part,
As faith ignites within the heart.
Guided by love, our spirits soar,
Embracing the blessings, we seek and explore.

Each step forward, a testament to grace,
In every challenge, we find our place.
Through trials faced, encouragement flows,
In unity together, our strength grows.

The sun ascends, our worries cease,
In surrendering, we find our peace.
The dawning light unveils the path,
Together, we bask in love's warm bath.

Hope is a beacon shining bright,
Guiding our souls through darkest night.
With gratitude, we lift our voice,
In the heart of faith, we rejoice.

Soaring with Purpose

Like eagles rising on winds of grace,
We seek the skies, our rightful place.
The spirit stirs, igniting the flame,
With vision clear, we call His name.

Purpose unfolds in every heart,
Each struggle faced, a sacred part.
With passion burning, we chase the dream,
Together united, a vibrant team.

In service and love, we find our call,
Lifting others, we will not fall.
In the depths of darkness, we shine so bright,
Illuminating the path with holy light.

From valleys low to mountains high,
We journey forth, our spirits fly.
Each act of kindness, a sacred thread,
Weave love and hope, where we're led.

Soaring above, we rise and sing,
In the heart of faith, we find our wings.
With every heartbeat, purpose grows,
In love's embrace, our essence glows.

Together we soar, hand in hand,
Embracing the gift of this wondrous land.
With courage bold, we take our stand,
Soaring with purpose, as we've planned.

The Spiritual Uplift

In moments rare, when spirits collide,
A dance of divinity, hearts opened wide.
With each gentle touch, our souls intertwine,
In sacred connection, the light we divine.

We gather in harmony, voices raised high,
With praises and songs, we touch the sky.
In unity's embrace, our worries cease,
In the flow of grace, we find our peace.

With arms outstretched, we feel the tide,
Love's gentle current, our faithful guide.
With wisdom shared, we feel the shift,
In every heartbeat, a spiritual uplift.

We walk the path laid out so clear,
Transformed by love, with courage, no fear.
In every prayer, we find the way,
In gratitude's light, our hearts will stay.

Together we rise with joyous delight,
Embracing our strengths, embracing the fight.
For in every challenge, we are reborn,
In the tapestry of life, true love is worn.

With voices united, we chant and cheer,
In the spirit of hope, we draw ever near.
A community blessed, together we lift,
In every gesture, the greatest gift.

Awakening to Grace

With each new dawn, our hearts align,
In the stillness, divine design.
As whispers of wisdom guide our way,
We awaken to grace, come what may.

In the dance of life, we find our place,
With gentle spirit, we embrace grace.
With eyes wide open, we see the light,
In each moment, the sacred feels right.

We gather our dreams, like stars in the night,
Illuminating paths with pure delight.
As laughter echoes, our souls take flight,
In the cradle of love, we hold on tight.

Through trials we grow, the spirit's call,
In every setback, we'll rise and enthrall.
We trust in the journey, a map drawn by fate,
Embracing the lessons that never abate.

With every heartbeat, we cherish each grace,
In love's gentle touch, we find our space.
Together, we walk, hand in hand intertwined,
In the beauty of grace, our souls are aligned.

In moments of silence, we hear the voice,
Awakening spirit, our souls rejoice.
Through the ebb and flow, forever we chase,
In the arms of love, awakening to grace.

Milton Keynes UK
Ingram Content Group UK Ltd.
UKHW020038271124
451585UK00012B/925